20th Century Inventions
LASERS

Nina Morgan

RSVP
RAINTREE
STECK-VAUGHN
PUBLISHERS
The Steck-Vaughn Company

Austin, Texas

20th Century Inventions

AIRCRAFT

COMPUTERS

THE INTERNET

LASERS

NUCLEAR POWER

ROCKETS AND SPACECRAFT

SATELLITES

TELECOMMUNICATIONS

Cover and title page: Laser beams fired into the sky from an observatory. The beams are part of a system that improves the view of the stars.

Published by Raintree Steck-Vaughn Publishers, an imprint of Steck-Vaughn Company

Library of Congress Cataloging-in-Publication Data
Morgan, Nina.
Lasers / Nina Morgan.
p.   cm.—(20th century inventions)
Includes bibliographical references and index.
Summary: Explains what lasers are and how they are used in communications, medicine, industry, and warfare, as well as possible future uses.
ISBN 0-8172-4812-9
1. Lasers—Juvenile literature.
2. Inventions—Juvenile literature.
[1. Lasers.]
I. Title. II. Series.
TA1682.M67   1997
621.36'6—dc20   96-44293

Printed in Italy. Bound in the United States.
1 2 3 4 5 6 7 8 9 0 01 00 99 98 97

Picture acknowledgments
Camera Press, 8 (right); Hulton Deutsch 9, Image Bank, 6/Robert J. Herko, 7/NASA, 21/R. Harris, 24 (bottom)/Alain Altair; Science Photo Library, *cover* and *title page*/Roger Ressmeyer, Starlight, 4/Lowell Georgia, 5/David Parker, 13/Volker Steger, 14/Philippe Plailly, 15/ Hank Morgan University of Massachusetts at Amherst, 17 (left)/NASA, 17 (right)/Philippe Plailly, 18/U.S. Dept. of Energy, 19 (top)/Santa Fe Technologies Inc., 19 (bottom)/Roger Ressmeyer, Starlight, 20 (top), 20 (bottom)/Dr. Jeremy Burgess, 22/Hank Morgan, 23 (left)/Philip Hayson, 23 (right)/Hank Morgan, 24 (top)/Eve Ritscher Associates, 26/Erik Viktor, 27/U.S. Dept. of Defense, 30/Lawrence Livermore National Laboratory, 31/Roger Ressmeyer, Starlight, 33/Michael Abbey, 34 (top)/Jerry Mason, 34 (bottom)/James King-Holmes, 35/U.S. Dept. of Energy, 37/Hank Morgan, 38 (left)/John Bavosi, 38 (right)/John Greim, 39/Alexander Tsiaras, 40/ESA, 42/ David Parker, 43 Imperial College; Spectrum Laser Systems 10 (both), 12, 32; Tony Stone Worldwide, 36/Rich LaSalle, 41/Michael Rosenfeld; TRH Pictures, 28/Hughes Aircraft, 29 (top)/CEV/Matra, 29 (bottom)/U.S. Navy; ZEFA 16. Artwork by Tim Benke, Top Draw (Tableau). All other pictures Wayland Picture Library.

CONTENTS

LIGHT FANTASTIC

Artists and filmmakers can use lasers for spectacular special effects.

The brilliant light shows at discos, the music that booms out of a CD player, the scanners that read bar codes at the supermarket checkout, and many types of computer printers all have something in common. They all depend on lasers.

When lasers were first invented in 1960, many scientists joked that they were a solution looking for a problem. Now it is hard to imagine life without the laser—they play a role in everything from astronomy to entertainment, from information storage to medicine, from surveying to pollution monitoring.

What are lasers?

The word laser is an acronym for the phrase "light amplification by simulated emission of radiation." A laser is a device for producing a type of light that is very different from the ordinary visible light we can see.

Visible light is made up of a mixture of wavelengths. The different wavelengths appear to us as different colors of light. What we see as white light is in reality a mixture of many different colors (see panel). In contrast, laser light is monochromatic, which means that it is made up mainly of one wavelength and appears to us as a single, very pure beam of color.

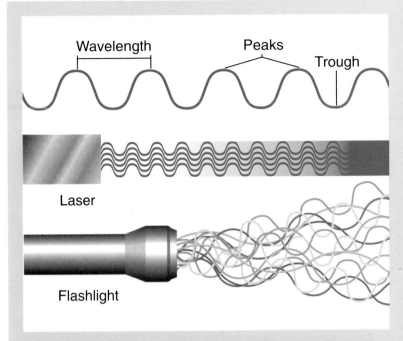

Wavelength   Peaks   Trough

Laser

Flashlight

A light wave (top). Laser light waves (middle) are in step with one another, and are all traveling in the same direction. Ordinary visible light waves (bottom) are out of step with one another, and move in many directions.

What is light?

Light is one of the many kinds of electromagnetic rays (energy-carrying rays) that the sun radiates, or gives out. Others include X rays, microwaves, radio waves, and heat. All types of radiation behave in many ways like waves. Waves are described by their frequency, which is the number of wave peaks or crests that pass a given point each second, and by their wavelength, which is the distance between peaks.

Light is a mixture of many wavelengths. Different wavelengths of light appear as different colors—violet, indigo, blue, green, yellow, orange, and red—which are seen in rainbows or when white light shines through a prism. Violet has the shortest wavelength and red has the longest. The other colors have wavelengths in between.

The light waves in visible light travel out of step with one another. Their peaks and troughs do not line up (see panel). Laser light is different. It is coherent. This means that in laser light most of the light waves are moving in step with one another, and traveling in the same direction.

Ordinary light waves spread out, or diverge, as they travel from their source. This explains why, when a flashlight is shined onto a wall, the spot of light that appears on the wall is much bigger and less bright, or intense, than the beam of light that leaves the flashlight. Laser light, on the other hand, does not diverge or become dimmer, even over very long distances.

A space shuttle can easily detect a laser beam targeted at it two hundred miles above Earth. Even over that huge distance, the laser beam spreads out only a little. Thanks to its coherence, intensity, and monochromatic nature, laser light makes spectacular displays at concerts and is used to light up the sky over cities on special occasions.

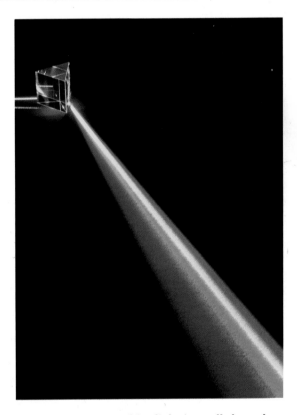

A prism separates white light into all the colors of the rainbow. Each color is made up of a different wavelength of light.

WHY ARE LASERS SO USEFUL?

Laser light is more than just spectacular. It is very useful, too. This is because the coherent light of a laser can be controlled very accurately. Scientists and engineers have found many different ways to take advantage of the special characteristics of laser light.

Lasers are becoming common tools in the operating room, where they can help doctors carry out operations quickly and safely.

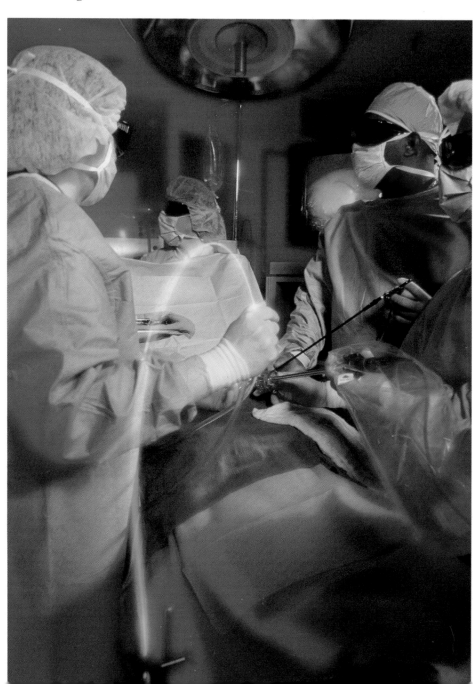

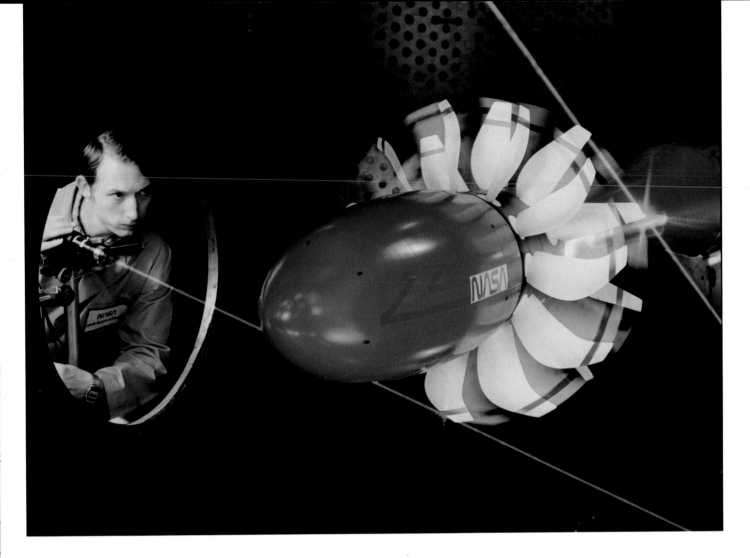

For example, because laser light is so intense, it is ideal for sending telephone messages and other types of data, or information, along fiber-optic cables. In these cables, signals travel as pulses of light through very fine fibers made of glass. The strong, nondivergent light beam from a laser also provides an ideal tool for marking out straight lines over long distances, as well as for measuring distances very accurately. Lasers also provide the source of coherent light needed to make holograms —pictures that look like three-dimensional images and appear different when viewed from different angles.

By switching them on and off very quickly, lasers can be used to apply large and very precise amounts of energy to very small areas. This makes them ideal tools for cutting, drilling, and welding. And by reflecting laser light off mirrors, the power of the laser beams can be used in places that are hard to reach. Since their invention in 1960, lasers have helped solve thousands of different problems in science, industry, and everyday life.

Lasers help scientists make very accurate measurements. Here a laser is being used to measure tiny movements in the moving blades of the fan. These movements would be difficult to measure accurately in any other way.

LASER PIONEERS

Although the first laser beam did not shine until 1960, the first steps toward the development of lasers took place long before. It began in 1917, when scientist Albert Einstein came up with the idea that it should be possible to stimulate, or encourage, atoms—the very tiny particles of matter—to make them emit (give out) light. But this idea turned out to be very difficult to prove. It took many years before scientists found a way to do it.

Above **Albert Einstein was the first person to suggest that it should be possible to stimulate atoms to make them give off light. He first talked about this idea in 1917, but it was not until 1960 that scientists finally found a way to do it.**

Right **Hungarian-born scientist Dennis Gabor first came up with the idea for taking three-dimensional photographs, or holograms, in 1948. He had to wait until lasers were available in the 1960s before his idea could become a reality.**

The breakthrough

The breakthrough came when three American scientists—
Charles Townes, James Gordon, and Herbert Zeiger—found
a way to excite atoms to make them emit not light, but
microwaves, another form of electromagnetic radiation
(see page 5). In 1954, they built the first maser (microwave
amplification by stimulated emission of radiation), a device
to produce a strong and controlled beam of microwaves.

This work encouraged many scientists to try to build lasers—
masers that emitted a beam of light instead of microwaves. The
first to succeed was American scientist, Theodore Maiman. On
May 15 ,1960, Maiman excited the atoms in a rod of the
mineral ruby, using a powerful flashlamp wound around the
rod, to produce the first laser beam. With this bright pulse of
deep red light, the age of lasers had begun.

Theodore Maiman (right), the
man who produced the first
laser beam. He carried out his
successful experiment in 1960,
and his work marked the start
of the age of lasers.

HOW LASERS WORK

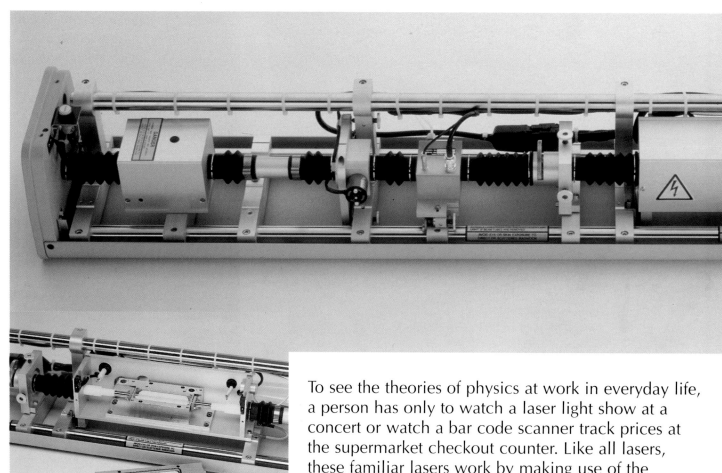

Top **The inside of a solid-state laser. Near the center of the laser is the pumping chamber, which houses the lasing medium. In this laser, a flashlamp is used to pump the lasing medium (inset). The laser light comes out on the left-hand side, where it passes through a series of lenses to focus it into a narrow beam.**

To see the theories of physics at work in everyday life, a person has only to watch a laser light show at a concert or watch a bar code scanner track prices at the supermarket checkout counter. Like all lasers, these familiar lasers work by making use of the physics of light.

Putting theory into practice

Lasers take advantage of the idea that light sometimes acts as a wave and, at other times, like a particle. The smallest unit, or fragment, of light is called a photon.

Photons behave like a particle and like a wave. Each photon carries a certain amount of energy. In a laser, atoms or molecules are made to release some of their photon energy as light. But before they can release energy, the atoms must first be stimulated, or encouraged, to move to a higher energy level. In a laser this is done by first inputting energy; for example, by turning on an electric current. This is called pumping the laser.

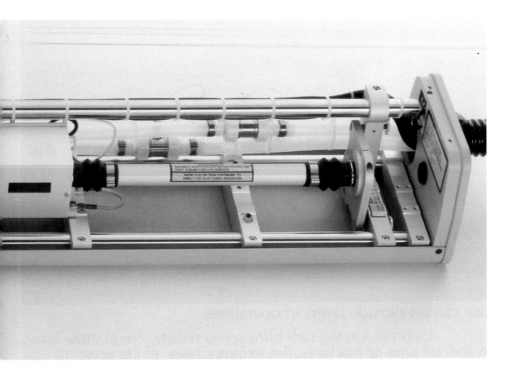

Below **The laser tube contains a lasing medium and has mirrors at both ends. When the laser is pumped, the atoms in the lasing medium become excited and begin to give off photons (top). The mirrors reflect the light back and forth. This causes more and more atoms to release light, until finally light emerges from an opening in one end of the tube (bottom).**

The extra energy pumped in is stored in the lasing medium where it is used to excite the atoms in the medium and cause them to move to a higher energy level. Because atoms always prefer to move toward lower energy levels, before long one of the excited atoms will release some energy by giving off a photon. When this photon strikes another excited atom, it causes it to release a photon as well. As more and more atoms are hit, they too release photons and light production grows. The mirrors at the ends of the tube help the process along by reflecting the light rays back and forth. This causes more and more excited atoms to release light.

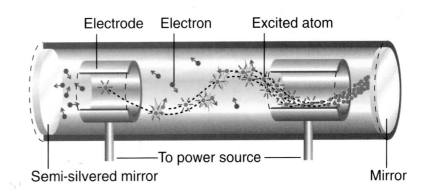

Electrode Electron Excited atom

To power source

Semi-silvered mirror Mirror

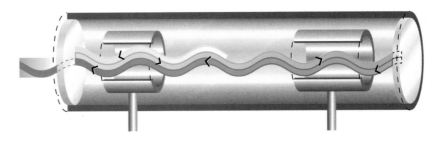

PACKING MORE POWER

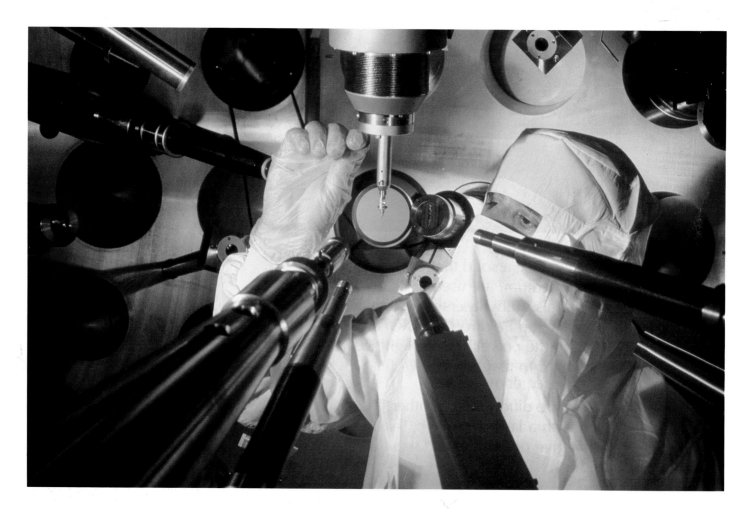

Very powerful lasers are used to explore the structure of atoms and to study fusion. Here a technician is positioning a target in a laser experiment that will study fusion.

Gas and semiconductor lasers produce their light in a continuous beam. This is known as continuous wave, or CW, operation. Other types of lasers, such as solid-state and excimer lasers, have a pulsed operation. Their laser light is produced in pulses.

Pulsed lasers can be made to give short pulses of higher power using the techniques of mode locking and Q-switching. In mode locking, powerful pulses are created by forcing all the photons in the lasing medium to move back and forth at the same frequency before the laser light is released.

A scientist carries out an experiment using a solid-state laser. Laser light can damage eyes, so he is wearing a dark safety visor to protect his sight.

In Q-switching, a shutter is placed between the lasing medium and a partially silvered mirror (a mirror that is not completely coated with a reflective material) at the end of the laser. This prevents the laser light from escaping and causes even more energy to build up in the medium. When the shutter is suddenly opened, the built-up energy escapes as a giant, high-energy pulse of light. The pulse lasts only a tiny fraction of a second, but it can pack a real punch. The power levels can be as high as several hundred thousand watts. An electric drill capable of drilling through stone walls only has a power of four hundred watts.

The most powerful lasers in the world

The most powerful lasers in the world are mostly used to explore the structure of atoms and for research into fusion (see page 34). These lasers emit very powerful pulses of energy—in the range of terawatts (million-million watts)—but the pulses are very short, measuring less than one picosecond (one million-millionth of a second).

In the United States, "Nova" (see page 30) produces up to ten terawatts. This laser uses glass as its medium.

MEASURING WITH LIGHT

A laser beam provides a straight line over a very long distance to help guide engineers when they are digging tunnels.

Measuring distance with light

Laser instruments use a microchip to record the time it takes for the laser beam to travel between the laser and the object. Then, knowing that light always travels at the same speed—186,000 miles per second—the distance to the object is calculated by multiplying the time by the speed of light.

Although all light travels in a straight line, laser light is especially good for marking straight lines because it is concentrated in a narrow, intense beam that is powerful enough to travel over very long distances without diverging, or spreading, very much.

Now, when engineers dig tunnels through mountains or under the waters of channels, they rely on laser beams to keep them on a straight course. Lasers are also helping shipbuilders to align very large pieces of ship's hulls to make sure they will fit together correctly the first time. When it comes to measuring very long and very short distances accurately, scientists, engineers, and factory workers increasingly find that nothing beats a laser.

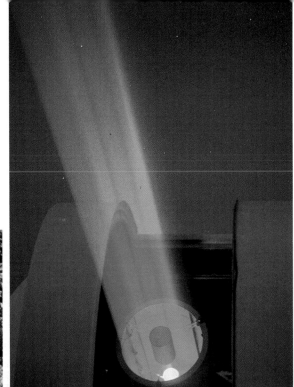

A laser beam (above) is directed toward reflectors on the surface of the moon (left) from a telescope in France. By measuring the time the beam takes to return to the telescope, scientists are able to calculate the distance to the moon to within two inches.

Measuring near and far

Surveyors use instruments called laser rangefinders that make very accurate measurements of distances, ranging from just a few feet up to about two miles. In a laser rangefinder, a laser beam is pointed at a reflective target. When the beam hits the target, it is reflected back to the rangefinder. The instrument records the time the beam took to make the round-trip and uses this information to calculate the distance to the target.

The same principles lie behind LIDAR, a type of radar that uses laser light rather than radio waves. In this system, pulsed laser beams are used to measure the distance of faraway objects. LIDAR has been put to some spectacular uses. In 1969, after American astronauts placed reflectors on the moon's surface, it was used to measure the distance to the moon to within just a few inches.

ON THE FRINGE

To measure very small distances, laser interferometers are the answer. These devices take advantage of another property of laser light: its coherence, or the fact that light waves move in step with one another.

In laser interferometry, a laser beam is split in two. Then one half is sent to reflect off one surface and the other to reflect off another. Because the two halves of the beam travel along different paths, when they meet again, they are slightly out of step. This produces a pattern of dark and light bands of light called interference fringes, which can be accurately used to figure out the distances between two objects.

Laser interferometers have many uses. In manufacturing, they are used to measure the thickness of very fine wires, or to check that parts made by machines are exactly the right size. Laser interferometers also help geologists to study earthquakes by keeping track of small movements along faults in the earth's crust.

Laser interferometry is a useful way of measuring very small distances. Here technicians are using a laser interferometer to measure the surfaces of several metal mirrors to make sure that they are perfectly smooth.

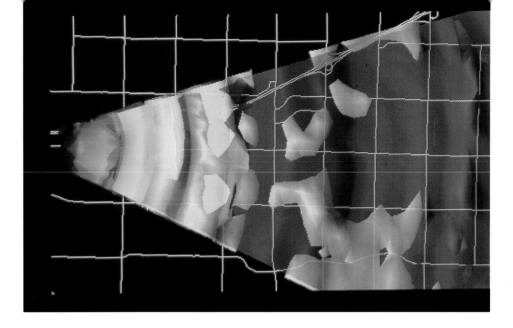

Scientists use laser beams to map out areas of pollution. In this air pollution map of the area around Albuquerque, New Mexico, the most polluted areas are shown in red and the cleanest areas are shown in blue.

An eye in the sky

Remote sensing satellites and airplanes gather information about things on the earth's surface. They work like spies in the sky to give a bird's-eye view of Earth. Some of the "eyes," or instruments, used to gather information are based on lasers. These take advantage of the fact that lasers can emit precise wavelengths of light that can travel over long distances.

By studying how these wavelengths are absorbed, or taken up, by chemicals in the air, scientists can measure levels of pollution in the atmosphere. Certain wavelengths of light make some chemicals give off light, or fluoresce. By using an airborne laser to shine the right wavelengths of light and then measuring the fluorescence, scientists can study subjects as different as the health of a forest or the size of an oil slick on the surface of the sea.

These laser beams measure small movements of the earth's surface on a volcano in California. This information will help scientists to predict when the volcano might erupt.

Watching the earth move

After the 1995 earthquake that caused serious damage in the city of Kobe, Japan, the Japanese government set up a network of laser-based stations, called Keystone, to keep a close watch on earth movements around Japan. Keystone will bounce laser beams off satellites orbiting the earth in an attempt to discover how the different stations are moving in relation to one another. They hope the information will help them to predict when an earthquake will occur.

INFORMATION AND COMMUNICATION

Lasers are used to both write and read information from compact discs to reproduce very high quality sound.

The amount of all our information, or data, is growing every day, but thanks to lasers, so is the means to handle it. Laser beams can be used to store and read information, reproduce sounds, and send more data through telephone lines.

Storing sounds

Laser technology makes your favorite bands sound as if they were in the same room with you. Compact discs (CDs) reproduce the very best in high fidelity sound by using lasers to first write and later read precise information about sounds.

On a CD, sounds are stored in the form of a series of digital data—patterns of zeros and ones. Digital recording, as this is called, not only accurately reproduces sounds, but also makes it possible for recording engineers to edit or change the recording using a computer to get the best sound balance and to produce special effects.

Because it is easy to index digital information, digital recording makes it simple for recording engineers to find exactly the part of music or sound they want to work on, and for listeners to home in on the track they want to hear.

A highly magnified picture showing the surface of a compact disc

Pits and flats

On a CD, sounds are recorded as a pattern of pits and flat areas on one surface of a metal-covered plastic disk. A laser beam from a tiny semiconductor laser is used to cut the patterns.

To listen to the sounds, the CD is placed on a CD player with the pattern of pits and flats face down. The player spins the CD around at a high speed, while a low-powered laser beam is focused on the CD's surface. When the beam hits a pit, it is scattered. But when it hits a flat, it is reflected back to a detector to produce a signal. This signal is a code for the recorded sound. Electronic circuits in the player change the signals into electric current, which is sent to the loudspeaker and changed into sound for listeners to hear.

The mixing board in a recording studio, where recording engineers mix all the sounds together to improve their quality

WORDS,
PICTURES,
AND SOUND

An artist uses a laser printer to print out a high-quality picture from a computer screen. Inside the printer, a laser beam is used to etch out a mirror image of the picture onto a photocopier drum. This image is then transferred onto paper.

The same type of laser technology is also used for videodisks. These disks record video pictures and sounds for later play-back on a television screen.

CD-ROMs (Compact Disk Read Only Memory)—disks that store words, pictures, sounds, and computer data are also made in this way. CD-ROMs are read using CD drives in computers. These use a low power semiconductor laser to read the patterns of pits and flats in a similar way to a CD player.

Space scientists use CD-ROMs to store the huge amounts of data gathered from satellites and space missions for later analysis and study. Now publishers are finding that CD-ROMS offer an exciting new way to present interactive books. These are complete with pictures and sounds along with words. By using a mouse to click on highlighted words on the computer screen, readers are taken quickly to other parts of the disk that contain related information.

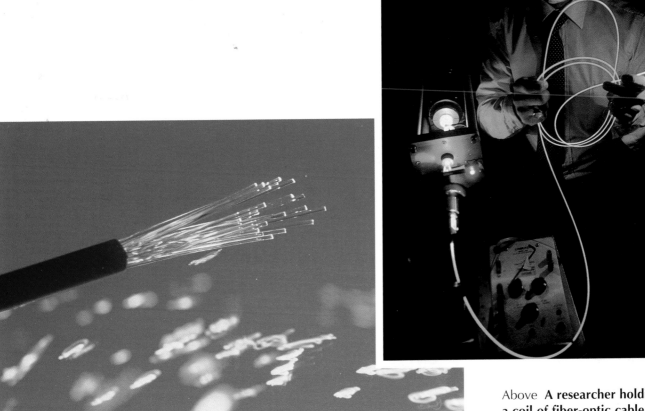

When it comes to printing words from a CD-ROM onto paper, lasers can also help. In laser printers, a laser beam is used to etch a mirror image of text or pictures on a photocopier drum. The drum is coated with a positively charged film sensitive to light. Wherever the laser beam etches, the drum takes on a negative charge. To make a paper copy, the drum is dusted with negatively charged toner, which sticks to all the places the laser has not touched. When a sheet of paper is run through the machine, the pattern of toner is transferred to the paper. Hot rollers then fuse the image to the paper to produce the printout.

Optical fibers

As more and more people use telephones and fax machines, lasers again come to the rescue. Fiber-optic cables, which carry signals in the form of pulses of different intensities of laser light, can carry many more calls than the ordinary copper wires used in telephone lines. In fiber-optic telecommunications networks, a single glass fiber can carry thousands of telephone calls at the same time.

Above **A researcher holding a coil of fiber-optic cable. No matter how the cable is bent, the light always travels down the cable and comes out at the end.**

Left **This cable is made of optical fibers. These thin glass fibers carry signals in the form of pulses of laser light. Fiber-optic cables make it possible for telephone lines to carry thousands of telephone calls at the same time.**

ADDING A NEW DIMENSION

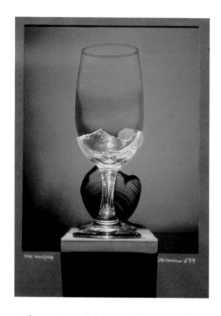

When viewed from different angles, this hologram of a broken wine glass looks like a whole glass.

In 1948, American scientist Dennis Gabor came up with an idea for taking a three-dimensional photograph, or hologram, of an object by splitting a beam of coherent light. When he had his idea, there was no way to produce coherent light. But once lasers came on the scene in the 1960s, holography became possible.

Now holograms seem to be everywhere. Some, like those on stickers, key rings, and magazine covers, are just for fun. Others have a more serious purpose. The holograms used on credit and bank cards are for security—they are difficult to copy, which makes cards forged by criminals easy to spot.

One day holograms may be used in three-dimensional body scans to help doctors study patients, and we may all enjoy three-dimensional television, thanks to moving holograms.

Bar codes

Supermarket bar code scanners shine a low-powered beam of laser light onto the bar code—a series of black and white stripes printed on the product's package. When the beam hits a black stripe, it is absorbed, but when it hits a white stripe, it is reflected back to a detector. This produces a pattern of signals that a computer uses to identify such information as the product name and price. This information is used to produce a total for the customer to pay. Bar codes also help supermarkets keep track of the number of items that have been sold and, when supplies get short, order new stock from the warehouse.

A laser scanner reads a bar code at a supermarket

24

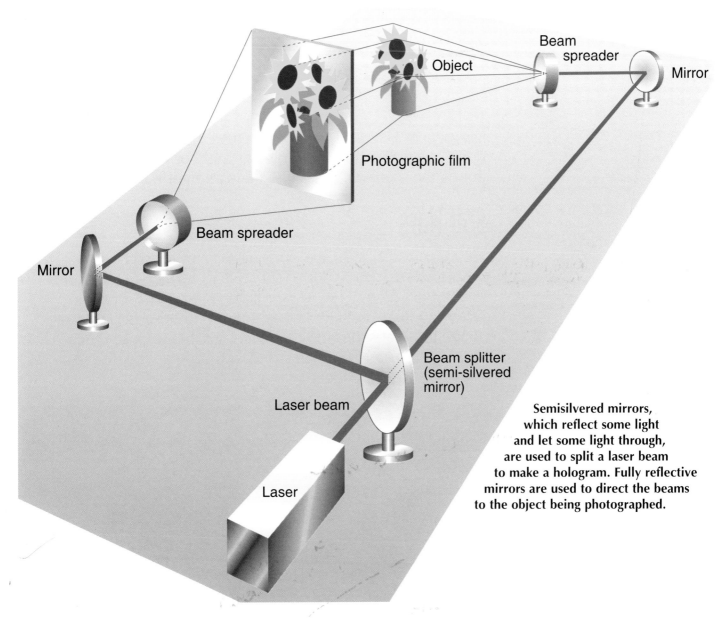

Beam spreader

Mirror

Object

Photographic film

Beam spreader

Mirror

Beam splitter
(semi-silvered
mirror)

Laser beam

Laser

Semisilvered mirrors,
which reflect some light
and let some light through,
are used to split a laser beam
to make a hologram. Fully reflective
mirrors are used to direct the beams
to the object being photographed.

Making holograms

Holograms are made by splitting a laser beam and directing each part of the beam onto photographic film from a different angle. When the two parts of the beam meet, they produce interference fringes, which look like tiny patterns of light and dark areas. These interference fringes are recorded on film to make the hologram. Some holograms, called reflection holograms, can be viewed in ordinary light. Others, known as transmission holograms, can only be seen using laser light.

LASERS AT WAR

Lasers were first used on the battlefield in the 1970s, when U.S. troops used them to guide missiles and bombs to their targets during the Vietnam War. Now they are important military tools.

Star Wars

For many years, laser weapons were favorites with science-fiction writers. Then, during the 1980s, science-fiction lasers seemed to come to life in the United States. The Strategic Defense Initiative (SDI), known to most people as Star Wars, aimed to put a series of laser-carrying satellites into space. The idea was to use laser beams to destroy enemy missiles soon after they were launched.

A drawing showing a laser weapon being fired from a space shuttle to destroy an enemy satellite

A *Titan 1* missile is destroyed by a laser during an SDI program test. The laser took several seconds to destroy its target.

Although the SDI program was canceled in 1993, the idea of using airborne lasers to attack missiles lives on. The U.S. Air Force is studying the possibility of carrying missile-destroying lasers on jumbo jets. The powerful lasers would be able to destroy enemy missiles from hundreds of miles away.

However, these laser weapons are still far in the future. To build them would require compact, portable lasers more powerful than anything so far developed.

Homing in

Laser guns are used by soldiers, but not for shooting at enemy targets. Instead, they help soldiers to determine distance to a target very accurately. Laser rangefinders are fitted to guns and other weapons to give them greater accuracy. The rangefinders work by sending out short pulses of laser light. These bounce off the target and are reflected back to a sensor on the rangefinder. The distance to the target is then calculated based on the time it takes for the beam to return.

BLINDING AND MARKING TARGETS

Low-powered laser weapons are used to disable missile-guiding sensors so that they no longer work. To do this, the laser weapons hit the sensors with a concentrated, low-powered beam of laser light. Even if the light beam is not powerful enough to damage the sensor, it can dazzle it so that it cannot "see" properly—just as bright headlights at night can dazzle drivers and make it difficult for them to see.

A soldier aims a laser designator. The laser guides missiles straight to their target.

Laser-guided bombs are released by a Jaguar combat aircraft of the French air force (above). The bombs destroy targets on the ground with pinpoint accuracy (right).

Antisensor weapons are often powerful enough to damage the eyes of soldiers. Experts believe that they have also been used to dazzle enemy pilots, even though this is against all international laws. The thought that lasers could be used on the battlefield to blind enemy soldiers is so frightening that groups such as the Red Cross are campaigning for a ban on their use.

Making their mark

Lasers are useful tools for marking, or lighting up, targets. Laser beams can be used to mark a target, making it easier for attack aircraft to see where to drop bombs or aim missiles.

During the Gulf War in 1991, a new laser marking system was used. Tools known as laser designators fired a series of coded pulses to mark targets, so that they could be recognized by the sensors used to guide missiles.

NUCLEAR TESTING

For testing nuclear weapons, high-energy lasers offer an alternative to actually carrying out explosions. These lasers, which can have power outputs of up to many million megawatts, can be used to heat and compress nuclear fuels. This allows researchers to study how the weapons would work, without actually exploding them.

At the Lawrence Livermore Laboratory in California, a laser called Nova, one of the most powerful in the world, is being used to study fusion reactions that could be used in new types of nuclear weapons. American scientists now plan to build an even bigger laser for developing nuclear weapons.

A flash of light in the test chamber of Nova. A full-power burst from the laser makes a pellet of fuel give off enough energy for a tiny fraction of a second—long enough for fusion to take place.

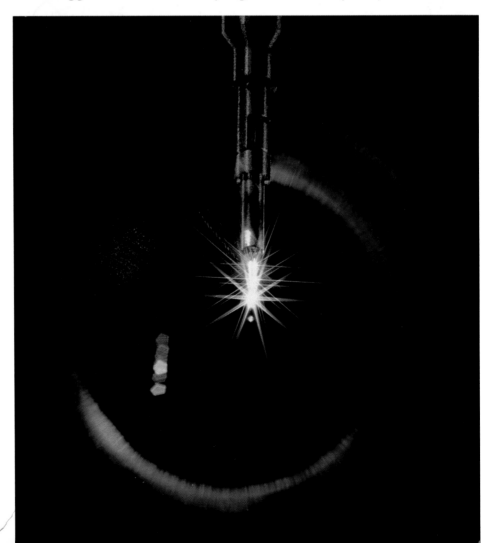

In one type of fusion experiment, ten powerful beams from the Nova laser are used to generate the very high temperatures needed to trigger a fusion reaction.

The new laser, known as National Ignition Facility (NIF), will be the most powerful laser ever built. It will be able to generate five hundred terrawatts of power for three billionths of a second, but will only be able to fire one laser shot every eight hours.

Protest in the Pacific

Lasers can help scientists to develop nuclear weapons, but they cannot completely replace nuclear testing. Researchers still need to calibrate their data by comparing the result of their experiments with data from real explosions.

When French scientists carried out underground nuclear explosions in the South Pacific in 1995, there were protests from people all over the world. But the French claimed that they needed to carry out the nuclear tests to calibrate their laser experiments.

SCIENCE AND INDUSTRY

Soon after they were invented in the 1960s, manufacturers realized that lasers could do many things that ordinary tools could not. In just a few years, lasers became known as the workhorses of industry. New uses for lasers are being developed all the time.

Flexible tools

Lasers are very flexible tools. Whether it is cutting and welding the huge metal plates used to build the hulls of ships or precision work, such as making a microchip, a laser is sure to be used. By just changing the way the beam is focused, it is possible to use the same laser for different kinds of jobs.

Lasers cut iron and steel by melting the metal. Because laser energy is so concentrated, only a very thin line of the material is melted. In laser welding, the intense heat produced by the concentrated light beam is used to melt and join the metals together.

A laser cuts through steel. The laser melts the metal as it cuts, leaving a smooth edge along the line of the cut.

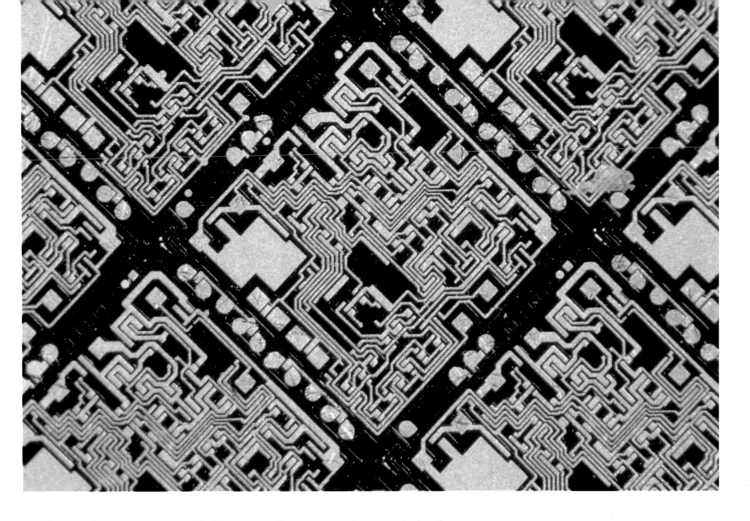

A silicon wafer contains several chips. Manufacturers use lasers to help them mark the tiny circuit patterns on the chips.

Precision power

In the microelectronics industry, lasers are hard at work performing tasks such as cutting precise shapes, micro-machining, drilling extremely small holes, or removing thin layers of materials—jobs that would be difficult, or even impossible, to do with any other tool.

Chip manufacturers use lasers to help them draw tiny circuit patterns on silicon wafers. They also use lasers as miniature welding tools to repair broken circuits and to "dope" chips. Doping means to stick in groups of different atoms at certain places on a chip's surface.

Just the job

The fact that there are so many different types of lasers available means that companies can choose the lasers that have the right power and emit in the right wavelengths to do the job at hand. Carbon dioxide lasers produce a continuous beam and are useful for jobs like cutting and welding steel. Carbon monoxide lasers have the right characteristics for working with plastics and ceramics. Copper vapor lasers produce a beam just right for working with aluminum, nickel, and copper—metals that are difficult to work with using other types of lasers. There is even a type of solid-state laser that can be used to bond together pieces of rubber and other waterproof materials without sewing them to make leakproof, waterproof clothes, boots, and wetsuits.

SHEDDING LIGHT ON SCIENCE

From astronomy to zoology, lasers are helping scientists gather new kinds of information in all branches of science.

Physicists are using short, powerful pulses from large lasers to study fusion reactions. These reactions could one day produce energy by causing certain types of hydrogen atoms found in seawater to fuse together and release energy.

Astrophysicists use very short, high-power laser pulses to copy the conditions found in the center of stars. This helps them in their study of the universe and its origins.

Above **This microscope uses a laser to light up these tiny soil-living worms (right).**

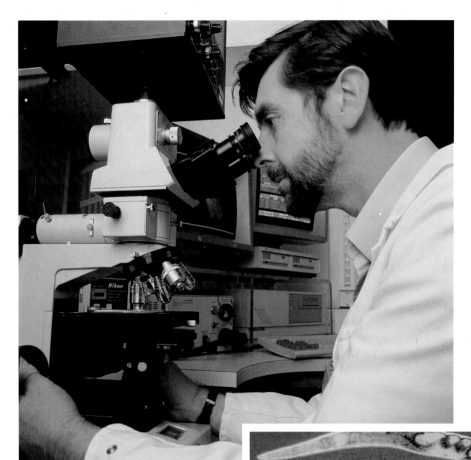

A scientist uses very fast flashes of laser light to study how coal ash particles flow. The flashes of laser light work like stop-frame photography to slow the movement of particles to make them easier to see.

Fast flashes

Flashes of laser light can work like stop-frame photography to slow the action and make fast-moving objects seem to stand still. Chemists and physicists can take advantage of incredibly fast laser pulses to see how atoms and molecules join to make new substances. In the future, it may even be possible to use ultrashort laser pulses to control the ways these reactions work. Biologists are benefiting, too. They are using the ultrafast flashes to study photosynthesis, the complicated set of chemical reactions that green plants use to capture energy from light.

Biologists are taking advantage of lasers to help them gain a clearer view of living things. In laser-scanning microscopes, laser light is used instead of ordinary light to light up the specimen. The light reflected off the specimen is recorded by a device known as a photodetector instead of being viewed through a lens. This information is processed by a computer to produce a picture of the specimen. Laser microscopes can be used to study objects as small as 0.1 micron (less than a millionth of a foot).

Laser light is also hard at work in chemistry laboratories. In laser spectroscopy, a pulse of light from a laser can vaporize, or turn into a gas, a tiny sample of a substance. The chemists then analyze the wavelengths of light the material absorbed or gave off. This information helps them tell what it was made of.

LASERS AND HEALTH

This tiny laser is used in surgery to make fine cuts through flesh. Lasers help reduce bleeding during operations. The laser beam heat seals the blood vessels as it cuts.

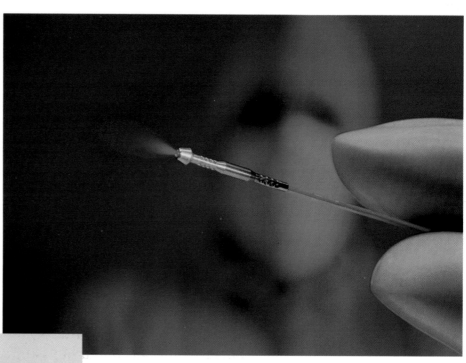

Curing without cutting

In some cases, lasers can even be used to prevent surgeons from having to make cuts at all. Lasers can break up hard, painful masses, called stones, that grow in the kidneys, and other organs are being tested. A small laser attached to an optical fiber is positioned inside the body near the stone. The laser produces pulses of power, which break up the stones into tiny fragments without harming the surrounding kidneys. The fragments are then passed through the body naturally.

Researchers are also working on new ways to use lasers to remove cancer tumors cleanly without damaging the surrounding healthy tissue. These types of treatments are much quicker and more comfortable for patients than traditional methods of surgery using scalpels.

Throughout the medical world, lasers are shedding new light on medical problems and how to solve them. In the operating room, lasers can replace scalpels and help doctors carry out delicate operations more safely, quickly, and effectively. Lasers also hold out the real prospect of painless visits to the dentist.

In traditional surgery, cuts are made with a sharp knife called a scalpel. But all cuts made with a scalpel bleed, and scalpels can be difficult to use in many parts of the body. Now surgeons have a new tool to treat their patients —the laser scalpel. This uses laser light focused to a fine pinpoint of heat to cut through flesh. The laser light is carried to the tip of the scalpel using optical fibers.

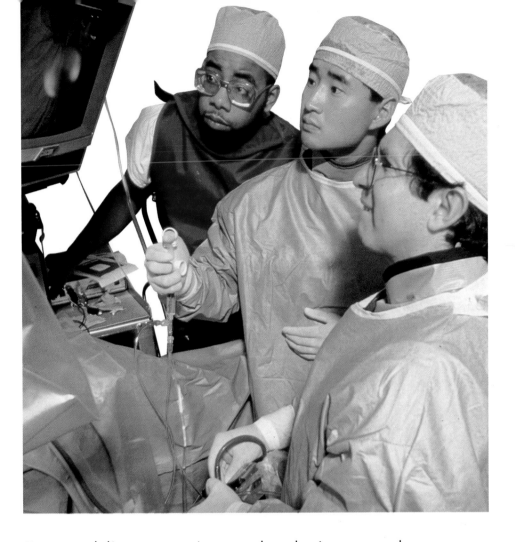

Doctors watch a video screen as a tiny laser fires pulses of light at a stone inside a patient's kidney. Tiny pieces of stone break off and later pass out of the patient's body.

For very delicate operations, such as brain surgery, laser scalpels can be used to make cuts much finer than a human hair. Laser scalpels also reduce bleeding during operations, because the heat from the laser beam cauterizes, or heat seals, the blood vessels as it cuts.

In control

To help serious burns heal, doctors must first remove the layers of burned skin to expose healthy areas, so that the rest of the skin can heal. A laser scalpel is a quick and relatively painless method of removing skin. Laser scalpels can also get rid of unwanted tattoos by removing a very thin layer of skin.

The power of the laser beam in the scalpel can be adjusted to make the scalpel useful for other jobs. At low power, the beam can weld together tears in tissues or leaking blood vessels. At high power, it can bore through or vaporize tissues. A high-powered beam is useful for clearing out blocked arteries or destroying unhealthy tissue.

EYE AND DENTAL TREATMENT

People using lasers must be very careful to wear special goggles to protect their eyes from laser light that can damage their eyes or even cause blindness. But properly used, lasers can be the eye's best friend. They can help repair eye damage, improve vision, and sometimes even restore sight—quickly and with little pain for patients.

For diagnosing eye diseases, scanning laser ophthalmoscopes allow doctors to study a patient's retina —the light sensitive coating of the eyeball. If the retina is damaged, a laser beam can be focused through the lens of the eye and used to repair small tears by welding them together. Lasers can also weld the retina back into place if it becomes detached from the back of the eyeball.

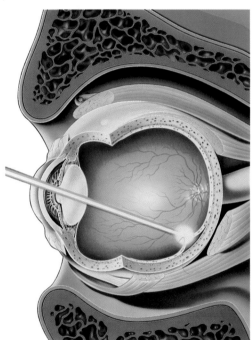

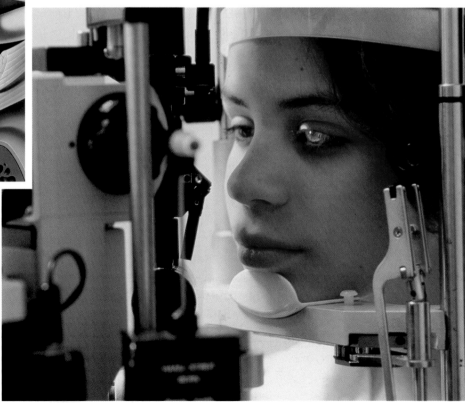

Right **A patient undergoing laser surgery on her eye. The diagram (above) shows how the laser beam reattaches the patient's retina (the light sensitive coating of the eyeball).**

To help people with poor eyesight see more clearly, lasers can be used to change the shape of the cornea, the outer transparent layer of the eye. In one type of treatment, an ultraviolet excimer laser is used to wear away the surface of the cornea. In another, the beam from a solid-state laser is used to shrink the thin outer layer of the cornea in order to change its shape.

At the dentist

Many people find that having a tooth filled is both nerve-wracking and painful. In addition, the fillings may only last about five years before they wear out and have to be replaced. However, in just a few years, going to the dentist for a filling could be a very different experience. Instead of drills, the dentist will use lasers to provide a painless treatment for filling cavities.

Using a beam of ultraviolet light from an excimer laser, dentists will vaporize only the decayed area—this type of drilling will not hurt at all. To prevent further decay, another laser will be used to kill any decay-causing bacteria before the hole is filled again.

The red aiming beam of a laser points to where the laser is vaporizing the decayed area of a tooth.

Bleaching birthmarks

Port wine stains are purple birthmarks caused by clusters of tiny blood vessels under the skin. These birthmarks can often be "bleached," or made to disappear, using lasers. For this treatment, the doctor chooses a laser that will emit the wavelength of light that is best absorbed by the patient's blood vessels. Usually copper vapor lasers or dye lasers are used. The energy absorbed from the laser causes a chemical reaction, which makes much of the color disappear.

LASERS FOR THE FUTURE

Where will laser development go in the future? Nobody really knows. But one thing is certain: the uses to which lasers can be put are limited only by people's imagination.

Cascading lasers

To make the most of the possibilities, the lasers of the future will have to be smaller, cheaper, and more powerful. They will also have to be more efficient at converting electrical energy into optical power. Today's lasers are amazingly poor at this.

Soon pulses of laser light from semiconductor lasers will be used to carry data between satellites orbiting in space.

One way to make lasers more efficient is to use lasers to pump other lasers. This process is known as cascading. Normally, electrical discharges, or flashlamps, are used to pump lasers.

Cascading is done by using a chain of tiny semiconductor lasers to pump energy into another laser. One after the other, each semiconductor laser in the chain pumps extra energy into the laser being cascaded. The more lasers added to the chain, the more the efficiency is increased. Including two or three semiconductor lasers in the cascading chain could increase the efficiency of the original laser by up to 30 percent or more.

Lasers being used to measure wind speed to test the wind resistance of a new car design

Optical tweezers

Although we cannot feel it, light actually pushes, or exerts pressure. Using lasers, scientists can take advantage of this weak pressure to create optical tweezers, which are powerful enough to move around and pick up tiny objects, such as single living cells in biology experiments.

To make optical tweezers, a small group of lasers that produce continuous beams are focused so that they create an intense circle of light. Inside the circle, the light pressure becomes powerful enough to be used as tweezers.

MORE CLEVER COMPUTERS

A researcher working on the Bit-Serial Optical Computer. This computer was built in 1993, and was the first optical computer. This type of computer contains no chips, but instead uses pulses of laser light to carry information.

Small is beautiful when it comes to computer chips. By finding ways to pack more electronic circuits onto a single chip, researchers hope to make it possible to develop more and more powerful computers. The lasers of the future will be able to help them.

Chips are made up of a thin wafer of silicon with electronic circuits etched into it. Pulses of laser light are used to transfer the patterns of the electronic circuits onto the silicon wafers. Today, it is possible to produce chips that are around a quarter of a micron (around a millionth of a foot) long. But to build faster and more powerful computers for the future, even smaller chips will be needed.

Femtoflashes

Researchers are finding ways to create shorter and shorter pulses of light. Now lasers have been developed that can generate pulses that last for only a six or seven femtoseconds (a few thousand-million-millionths of a second). Faster flashes from lasers will make it possible for even more telephone calls and data to be carried through a telephone line —and at greater speed, too.

A dye laser system set up to produce flashes of light that last for only a few femtoseconds.

One way to do this is to develop lasers that emit shorter pulses of light at shorter wavelengths, such as blue. Using these pulses of blue light, it will be possible to transfer even finer patterns of circuits onto the chips.

Optical computers

Another way to build more powerful computers is to do away with chips altogether, and build optical computers. In these computers, light pulses from a laser will carry the information. The pulses will be directed and controlled as they travel through the circuit using tiny mirrors. Because light travels much faster than electronic signals, optical computers will add speed, as well as power, to computers. For some uses, chips and electronic circuits could one day become a thing of the past.

DATE CHART

1917 Albert Einstein suggests that it should be possible to stimulate atoms to make them give off light.

1948 Dennis Gabor has the idea of splitting a beam of coherent light to make a three-dimensional photograph or hologram, but no source of coherent light is available.

1954 Charles Townes, James Gordon, and Herbert Zeiger build the first maser, a device that gives off a strong, controlled beam of microwaves.

1960 On May 15, Theodore Maimen tests the first successful laser and produces the first laser beam.

1961 Leon Goldman, a dermatologist (skin specialist) in Ohio, uses a ruby laser to lighten a port wine stain birthmark.

1961 Charles Campbell, a doctor in New York, uses a laser to weld a detached retina to the back of a patient's eyeball.

1962 American General Curtis LeMay suggests that lasers might be a good weapon against ballistic missile attacks.

1963 C. Kumar and N. Patel, working at Bell Telephone Laboratories, introduce a new type of laser: a carbon dioxide laser for use in industry.

1965 Experiments carried out on mice by a doctor in Boston seem to show that laser light can kill cancer cells without killing surrounding tissues. Now doctors are not so sure that lasers are able to do this.

1965 The first chemical lasers, pumped by the energy of a chemical reaction rather than by energy from outside sources such as light and electricity, are tested.

1965 The company North American Aviation (now part of Rockwell) builds a neodymium-doped glass laser that fires up to 60 pulses per second and can drill holes as small as 0.01 millimeters in titanium sheets.

1966 Scientists Frantisek Hoff and Rudolf Konvalinka demonstrate the first successful transmission of a laser beam over a distance of three miles. Now laser beams travel much greater distances—even into space.

1968 An argon laser is first used by an American doctor to cut membranes in the eye. The operation improves the sight of two of his patients.

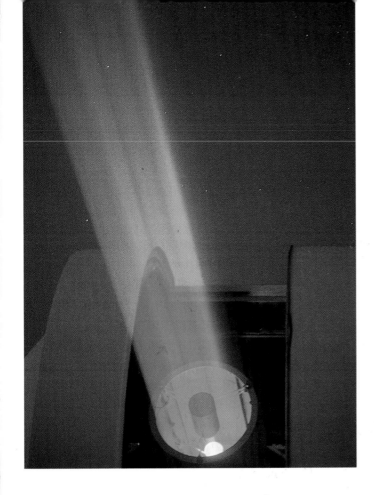

1969 August 1, scientists use a laser to measure the distance to the moon. The laser light was reflected back to Earth from a reflector placed on the moon's surface by astronauts.

1970 Flashlamps with a lifetime of one million shots are developed. These are used to pump solid-state lasers.

1971 Carbon dioxide lasers first used in surgery to remove papillomas, fast-growing warts that can grow in the throat, head, and neck.

1972 Laser rangefinders and target designators (markers) are first used on the battlefield in Vietnam.

1978 The U.S. Navy uses a four hundred kilowatt chemical laser to shoot down an antitank missile.

1978 The U.S. Navy begins work on a 2.2 megawatt giant chemical laser known as MIRACL.

1978 The U.S. Air Force sets up an Airborne Laser Laboratory. This consists of a four hundred kilowatt gas-dynamic laser carried in a military version of a Boeing 707 airplane. The laboratory is not a success. In 1981, it failed to shoot down a ground-to-air missile in tests.

1983 The Star Wars program, which aims to put a series of laser-carrying satellites into space, begins.

1991 Laser designators, or target markers, are used in the Gulf War.

1993 The Star Wars program is canceled.

INDEX